Intelligent Legendary Leaders
The Tru Souljahs diary
&
The Revenge of Makaveli

By: Qa'id Walker-Teal

This is dedicated to my fallen Tru Souljah Unique Berring. I Love You!

Acknowledgments

I first give all my honor & glory to God because without You there's no me. This book came from the bottom of my heart in hopes that it reaches yours. I also want to send a special thank you to the village of Tru Souljahs who raised me to become what I am today but most importantly thank you for the man I shall become. A special thanks goes to my father and mother. I can't thank you enough for the way you raised me. I promise to show the world you didn't raise another statistic. Last I want to thank every person that discredits my character in any way. I don't have my life together but how many 20 year olds you know have it all together, the least you could do is give me credit for trying to be the best I can be. Much Love, Peace, & Positivity; may God bless.

Table of Intelligence

Preface

The intelligent legendary leader is simply a diary that was created for my Tru Souljahs. A quick read on mind elevation and connecting to a higher purpose.

I.L.L

"The human mind is magnificent in many ways. First and foremost important being that the human mind is controlled only by itself. Therefore my life and the life of everyone on planet earth sums up to be the end equation of their mind. In better sense you are the human form of your mind."

Qa'id Walker-Teal

Energy

Everything around us is made of matter. Matter is the substance in which any physical object consists or composed of. In order to sustain matter it needs constant flow of energy. Energy in return keeps matter moving. Everything that is tangible is made of matter and needs energy. Remember how I mentioned that you equal the sum of your mind. Turns out that our mind is the world's most powerful source of energy. Allow me to elaborate! Everything physical is made of matter. Matter needs energy to move and the human mind is the most powerful source of energy. Therefore your mind is the matter that makes the world move. YOU ARE THE UNIVERSE!

Energy has three important forms; positive, negative, and karma. Negative energy simply put is the bad energy in all forms (hate, envy, distrust, etc.). Positive energy on the other flip of the coin is the complete opposite (love, loyalty, trust, etc.). Then there's karma!

Karma is the positive or negative energy that you send out into the world that boomerangs back to you. Your thoughts, actions, and intensions; good or bad will determine your karma.

Everything around us is made of energy. That means any and everything has a positive or negative effect on our life. From the company you keep, to the music you listen, all the way down to the food you consume. Everything about us has a flow of energy, so it's best to flow as much positive energy as possible because one thing is for sure that what you give off comes back to you.

The Power of a Dream

"A major part of life is building a life that you can live with."
-Dizzy Wright

Imagination happens to be the driving force that has advanced life, as we know it. Many adults lose this trait transitioning from children to adults being hit with harsh realities of life. The Tru Souljah learns to maintain imagination and understand that the life they want to live is never given it's only earned. Your dreams & goals mean something let no one tell you different. You have a God given purpose that you must fulfill by any means. There's a reason you face the battles you face; there's a reason certain people are toxic to you; there's a reason you love the people you love; and most importantly there's a reason you think and dream the way you do. You're very special in many ways and the only point of life is finding at least one gift. Master that gift and figure out how to get paid for it.

The power of a dream is key, pay attention! The Tru Souljahs' dream simply put is an idea of a picture perfect life. As humans we have a natural tendency to seek better life. An ideal picture perfect life ultimately is a thought. Your thoughts are your most *powerful source of energy because that's the only thing in this universe that is controlled by you. In addition your thoughts (good or bad) turns into your actions. Your daily actions (good or bad) will determine your future self. Life is filled with challenges, everyone has their own. So through every battle program your mind to believe every win and lost is a lesson learned.*

Mastery

Growing up I'm pretty sure many adults slurred to you that life is hard. I want to be the first to tell you LIFE IS NOT HARD. Life is and always will be what you make it. The major key is understanding. The Tru Souljah knows that the only person that needs to believe in you, is yourself. Whatever you imagine your life to be, can happen but only through self esteem. Self-esteem is confidence in one's own worth or abilities. You then must build a furnace in your belly filled with burning desire and hunger to carry out your mission. After that you have to have a why. In other words, what's your purpose? In Life everything that happens has a reason. On the same coin so does your dreams.

I was always told you must live for something or you will fall for anything. The true art of success is mastery. You must master one's self; conquer all weakness and master all strengths. Mind over matter. Then master one's soul; higher self over lower self. Last but not least master one's body; maintain a healthy diet and daily workout plan. This plot can work for anyone with the brain capacity to understand the words in this book. The only way for it to work is through self-discipline, which happens to be a characteristic that no one is born with, it can only be told or taught to you through trial and error.

Emotions

"...No matter how hard it get, stick yo chest out, keep your head up, and handle it."
-Tupac Shukar

  To become a master of emotions, you must fully understand that life comes with challenges. Everyday is not promised so today is a blessing. If you live your purpose that's all God could ask of you.

  Every obstacle is a lesson needed for the person you wish to become. Always remember after every thunderstorm comes a beautiful rainbow, so smile through the rain and watch the storm fade to glory. The only person that can fight the battles you face is the Tru Souljah you see in the mirror. Pops always told me nobody can love me like I love myself and no one can believe in my dreams until I love

my dreams enough to make them come
true.

Negative Emotions

Fear, anger, frustration, anxiety,
sorrow, and disappointment are
negative emotions that everyone faces.
A master of emotions will learn to
reverse the negative energy and turn it
into fuel for success. Every negative has
an opposite we call positive. Turn fear
into fierce, turn anger into admiration,
turn frustration into encouragement,
turn anxiety into composure, turn
sorrow into joy, and turn
disappointment into success. Very much
easier said than done, but your self-love
will give you discipline to master your
emotions.

Self-Love

Until you love yourself, you can
never fully love anyone else. Love comes
with sacrifices. The Tru Souljah must
sacrifice the person you are today for
the person you shall be. Love yourself

enough to always go the extra mile. Whatever you do, do it with the best of your abilities and aim to do it better than ever before. The history of success is only a blueprint on how it was done; the Tru Souljahs purpose is to make it better. Love for yourself will help you gain habitual habits of success. Love yourself enough to gain self-discipline. The Tru Souljah understands that in order to be a Tru dream chaser takes consistency & hard grit, with a mindset that nothing or no one can stop you but you.

Finding God in the Tru Souljah

"Imma slave in my mind but I know God, so I'll be where I wanna be in no time... I had a vision now I'm living the proof"

-Dizzy Wright

To truly find God; you must find yourself. Every religion has a set of beliefs set by its founders. God is the creator; His name differs through religion. If you notice the common factor in majority of religion is that God is high and any wrongdoing is low. That's the message. God is in the Tru Souljah. You have a higher self hence a lower self.

Since birth we're all conditioned on what's right and wrong. The only way to connect with the most high is by doing what your spirit says is the right thing to do. Losing track and doing things you know are wrong is when God sends the Tru Souljah a personal storm of trails and tribulations. Only for us to live and learn, but most importantly get back in line with the God in the Tru Souljah. The choices we make are vital. In every decision there's a good or bad choice. A lot of times we fall simply because we make decisions on instinct rather than thinking thoroughly for the best solution.

The Revelation of Jesus Christ

On the 19th day of August 2017, black Jesus was secretly killed. He was slain execution style by the head on the island of Cuba and placed on the seal of the two headed ghetto bird. The wrath of Afeni shook all 4 corners of the earth. Pain, judgement, and all-out war effected a whole universe of people. It was a beautiful battle cry as Our Lord and savior ascended from the heavens and scanned over a nation of hate and unrighteousness 3 days later on the 21st of august. All eyes on the most high as the solar eclipse stunned the nation of lady liberty. Hail Mary to Makaveli and the unveiling of Black Jesus.

The last days are done when the battle of Love is won. Time and time again we've been lied to and manipulated from the truth. The real truth is the universal God that created our world resides in the sun, the mother is the moon, and her children are the bright stars in the sky. To be Godly we must purify our mind, body, and soul with things from the universe because that's what universal people are made of. Atoms dwell within the entire universe and even more so within ourselves. The tru Kingdom of heaven shines from within. The more we nurture the God in us, the better off our world would be on the outside.

The Tru Souljahs Prayer

I am a child of God; with Him I stand in battle. I fear no man for He is the only master... Anything my mind can conceive, I shall achieve. For I am a child of God, with Him I stand in battle. I keep my head on straight with a big smile on my face, because I am a child of God, with Him I stand in battle. "Every obstacle means possible even when winning is illogical, losing is still far from optional" for I am a child of God; with him I stand in battle. I am created in His image for his power is within me, I am a child of God, and with him I stand in battle. I shoot for the stars with the intent to catch them all, and I pray for my enemies they shall never defeat me; my dear Lord will always defend me, because I am a child of God with Him I stand in battle.

Riches Or Wealth

Once you accumulate a plan you then must put all your time & effort into completing the Tru Souljahs God given mission. You have 24 hours every blessed day you wake up. How you spend that time determines how close you are to your dreams. Time waits for no man so every moment you spend not chasing your dreams becomes a day without them coming true.

In Today's time you need financial freedom to truly be free. It's highly important for you to understand the difference between riches and gaining wealth. Having riches is being able to provide for yourself during your time on earth but true wealth is being able to provide for future generations once your time is up. Even though riches and wealth differ they also have a big common factor (Success). Success is being able to do what you want, go where you please, buy what you want, and provide for yourself and those you love.

Multiplying Military Minds

It's a true token that teamwork makes the dream work; so to be an intelligent legendary leader you must always put your team first. When you have a purpose, it's highly beneficial to align your mind with the minds of those in the position you wish to be in. The Tru Souljah must always remember association brings about assimilation meaning you are the company you keep. In todays time the margin for success has only gotten greater, simply because we have mass numbers of information through technology. The birth and improvement of the World Wide Web has unlocked unlimited information and making self-education limitless. It's nearly impossible to search the Internet and not find what you are looking for. With that being said, the base blueprint is already written and 9 times out of 10 it's on your cellphone at your fingertips.

When you really want success bad enough it will become second nature. You start by dreaming up God's plan, then make it your every thought, after that align yourself with successful people & successful habits. Success is not easy but that doesn't mean impossible. You are what you say you are and your team reflects what you stand for. The art of multiplying military minds is finding like-minded Tru Souljahs with similar goals that add positive energy and benefit your future success.

Hustle Habits

A Tru Souljah must always stay true to oneself and true to those around you. To truly be rich is to be rich in spirit. Money is tangible and is only needed for your time on earth, so your chosen hustle must reflect what you stand for. Life comes with many challenges so its key to always try your best to do the right thing even when no one is watching. Your positive input continues your positive output, creating a more positive mind. A free positive mind allows a Tru Souljah to be better suited for any battle. When a battle seems too tremendous a Tru Souljah understands the greatest warfare is strictly for the greatest Souljahs.

The ambition of a Tru Souljah speaks without words being spoken. Simply because you only find Tru Souljahs in those who fall in love with their chosen craft. Once a souljah finds passion in purpose the only pressing concern becomes perfecting the craft & expanding the mind. The most important hustle habit of the Tru Souljah is the will to learn and evolve every blessed day. The Tru Souljah understands that time waits for no man, so time is spent either studying or perfecting the craft. Reading is truly a necessary hustle habit because it self-educates the Tru Souljah, enhancing the vocabulary by the same token improving speech and ability to speak professionally.

The last hustle habit of a Tru Souljah is the art of sitting still. A lot of times we get bored and impatient, but my mom always told me that boredom is the devils playground. Ironically we tend to make our dumbest mistakes out of boredom. The Tru Souljah knows that sitting still; being out the way from trouble, and constant mind elevation is the master key for success.

Against All Odds

Trials and tribulations are what make life a reality. If everything was picture perfect then no one will have the will to do better. The turns and bumps in the road make the road to riches all worth it. Overcoming adversity is what separates the strong from the weak. To be a Tru Souljah you must fully understand that your mind is P.O.W.E.R.F.U.L., powerful beyond measure. "The man who says he can and the man who says he can't, are both right."

Your mind controls everything about you and with your mind you control your destiny. Always Finish On Course Until Successful, F.O.C.U.S. Every battle is meant to bring out the better you. The pain you face is the weakness leaving the body. So with every battle God gives you, is simply a sacrifice and lesson needed for your future self. Under pressure is when a Tru Souljah is at thy best, control your mind, and never stress. No matter what, if you're breathing always give your best effort and then some. Never limit yourself through false events appearing real, F.E.A.R. So stand tall ten toes firm because every battle you beat is a blessing you earn.

Intelligent Legendary Leaders

To be a Tru Souljah you must be I.L.L. in everything you do. Your life is important so by any means necessary you have to give your best effort in every breathing moment. In the words of Dizzy Wright "Only you can slow you down, so turn your dreams into commitments". You only have one life to live and it makes no sense to live your whole life paycheck to paycheck. Life is *a struggle but struggle doesn't mean impossible. It's a fact that we all must live and learn how to maintain but the Tru Souljah learns to maintain thy dreams until they become reality.*

The art of being I.L.L. is simple. The Tru Souljah must first gain intelligence meaning thy must learn to use knowledge as power. Then the Tru Souljah must become legendary in chosen craft meaning thy must live for God's purpose. Finally the Tru Souljah must lead meaning thy must set the best example for future generations.

…You have in your hands everything you need to change your mind and change your life. Now the question becomes, "Do you want success as bad as you want to breathe"?

Tru Souljah Poetry

Still minds with humble drive
Still rise in due time. In Gods
eyes you will shine at the
perfect time. If you lack
patience and commitment you
become a bird with no wings
because a vision without
actions is merely a dream.
Plot the scheme to your
picture perfect dream, and
understand you blessed. When
trouble comes your way
there's no need to stress. As
long as God comes first then
this life's a test. Just stick yo
chest out and always stand 10

toes solid. If they bleed like
you then fear nobody

Tru Souljah Poetry

Humble headed hustla itching
for riches, making money
moves mandatory and God is
my witness. Imma Tru souljah
so I know I gotta grind to
grow, once I touch my goals
Im going to get some mo. I
keep my eyes on the prize,
watch the hate in disguise.
Always stay Tru to oneself
and never tell no lies. In the
very end only you can cause
yo demise.

Tru Souljah Poetry

Friends & foe's can leave you in the cold. Only you got yo back so you must stay on yo toes. Peep the smiles but always listen to the lies told. Never ever ever let someone kill yo glow. You have a purpose in this life it's a must you live it. If the vision is blurred you must hustle till it's vivid. Put some passion in your purpose till yo soul reach heaven and yo body in a hearse because that's the only reason for your birth.

"A Vision without actions is merely a Dream"...

.... Time to Fulfill Yours.

He who has an ear let him hear what the Lord has to say, take heed this bread and eat it, in hopes that it fufill your mind, body, and soul.

Made in the USA
Middletown, DE
19 May 2022